Our Traditions

COVINGTON WRITER'S GROUP

COVINGTON WRITERS GROUP

OUR TRADITIONS

SEPTEMBER 2016

Jenny Breeden, Managing Editor
Elle Mott, Assistant Editor
Gary Reed and Mikey Chlanda, Proofreading Editors

COVER ILLUSTRATION COPYRIGHT ©
COVINGTON WRITERS GROUP, INC.

Designed by Jenny Breeden

ISBN-13: 978-1945368035
ISBN-10: 1945368039

PUBLISHED BY
COVINGTON WRITERS GROUP, INC.
IN CONJUNCTION WITH
SEAGULL PRODUCTIONS LLC.
COVINGTON, KENTUCKY 41014

OUR TRADITIONS

FOR OUR FAMILIES AND FRIENDS

TABLE OF CONTENTS

ACKNOWLEDGMENTS

February 2016 marked the second anniversary of the Covington Writers Group (CWG). Anniversaries, as well as other special occasions, are usually celebrated in certain ways, commonly referred to as "Family Traditions". We noticed many of these traditions included a special family recipe or craft project, some of which have been passed down from generation to generation. We decided to share some of our favorite traditions and the foods or projects that make our stories unique. We hope you enjoy our personal recollections, sample some of our recipes or crafts and maybe add them to your own traditions. The CWG members would like to express their heartfelt thanks to the following:

- Family and friends, for allowing us to spend some of our time away from them while we write, share our work at group meetings and grow as writers. Their love and sacrifices mean the world to us as we strive for success.

- The Covington Branch of the Kenton County Public Library, John Graham, Gary Pilkington and the staff, for providing our meeting place on the first and third Saturday mornings each month, where we share our stories and writing ideas in a comfortable, state-of-the-art facility.

- Zola Pub and Grill and their staff in MainStrasse Village, for providing us with their spacious second floor dining area on the second and fourth Saturday evenings each month so we can socialize and critique stories in a friendly environment.

- The Left Bank Coffeehouse and their owners and staff on Seventh Street in Covington for providing us with coffee services for some of our group meetings and for our speaking seminars and writing workshops.

1 – BIRTHDAYS

LIFE LESSONS THROUGH CAKE

By James Ballard

Birthdays are inescapable events in everyone's life. They happen every year and don't care how young or old a person may be. Each birthday is different in its own way but there's generally one simple theme that comes with them, and that is the birthday cake: a customizable delicacy shared with friends and family during any celebration of birth. Though it didn't originate in America, it found its way here with time.

My family is no exception to this rule. Growing up, I had a cake on each birthday. Even when times were tough, we had some form of cake to celebrate. As a child, I looked forward to the cake with each approaching birthday. When I became a young man, I figured I had matured past cake, but when I almost went one birthday without it, I realized just how accustomed to it I was. In my case, I was lucky a friend made one for me, but that isn't the main story I wanted to discuss today.

The real story was the time when, with no experience in cooking, much less baking, I tried to make a birthday cake on my own.

My birthday falls in summer and on that particular day, it was exceptionally hot. Not looking forward to being a year older, I had been mildly dreading my birthday. I was already mad at myself for getting winded on a couple flights of stairs. I didn't want a reminder of my age, especially if the first two numbers matched my current weight at the time.

However time cares not for the opinion of mortals, and my birthday was coming up. I had been reminded by my family on multiple occasions that I was probably going to be spending it alone.

I wasn't sure how to respond to that situation, but in the end, decided to just do something for myself. If I was going to be spending it alone, I decided to try making myself a cake.

I usually had a plain vanilla cake but I wanted to go with something exciting, something that would tickle the senses and leave me both satisfied and regretful at the end. I got a Red Velvet cake mix because it was on sale.

I had never baked anything, much less made a cake before. My greatest cooking accomplishments were ramen noodles and hamburger which, using my natural skills as a cook, I topped with cheese. However I felt there was no point in thinking too hard about some things. Sometimes taking a leap is necessary to learn more about oneself in the world.

I didn't realize how badly this was all going to go.

Now, as anyone who's taken the time to make a cake knows, it's not incredibly complicated, although it can be a tad time consuming. I was home alone staring at my gas stove like a mother at a guilty child. I was preparing for an intense battle with a device I barely understood, but cooking a cake in a microwave wasn't an option. I went in with confidence— at least until I remembered that all I had was the cake mix. I needed the other ingredients!

I discovered there were instructions on the box. After looking up how many teaspoons equaled a tablespoon, I had my weapons for war. I had scouted, created a game plan and the only thing left was putting the plan into action. I grabbed a whisk and a bowl and went in with gusto.

I didn't succeed.

My cake came out far too fluffy. It felt like I was biting into a cloud with each bite. Apparently, I didn't mix long enough. It was just a mess. I had also completely forgotten to buy icing and candles, so it was a giant red circle that I stared at for ten minutes. The only thing I got right was the shape and that was barely.

At first, I was depressed at the thought that I had failed, and now I was going to be without a birthday cake. I told my grandmother about it and she laughed. I didn't understand initially but eventually I started laughing too, finding the humor in my failed attempt.

Allow me to share a lesson that perhaps you learned long before I did. The important thing about birthdays is the memory. The reason cake is so important is because it's a part of that memory. But the real important part is sharing that time with other people, whether it be on your own or another person's birthday.

Cake causes those memories to come back, especially if you have the same kind every year. If you see someone else's birthday cake, it reminds you of your last one and the fond memories that come with it.

I'm still practicing my cake baking skills and have a new respect for those that make them each year. I hope the next time you share your own cake with those close to you, you keep the memory close to your heart for the future.

Red Velvet Cake (Easy Version)

One box of Red Velvet cake mix and its ingredients:
- ½ cup vegetable oil
- 3 Eggs (I use two most of the time)
- Red food coloring
- 2 tablespoons of baking cocoa
- 1 cup of buttermilk or water

Directions:

The box may differ slightly in directions but the simplest way is to heat the oven to 350° F and grease the bottom (with a little vegetable oil from the bottle, of course). Toss the cake mix, eggs, oil, food coloring, cocoa, and buttermilk/water into a mixing bowl and beat it with a wire whisk and some elbow grease or an electric mixer, if you have one, for thirty to forty-five seconds or until it's all mixed together into one large goop.

Check the box on how long to bake it, but let it cool for about ten minutes— nine if you're feeling dangerous.

Don't forget the frosting (if you know how to make it, you can buy it at a store). Finally, pour the icing onto the cooled cake and smooth it out. Then dig in and commit to your diet another day!

SEPTEMBER BIRTHDAYS

By Patti Kay Emerson

When I was a child, September birthdays were like Christmas. That was because there were three of them, all in one week.

Because our birthdays were so close together, we always celebrated our birthdays together with just one bakery cake for the three of us. My sister, Mary, lived and worked in another city, so we had to arrange the celebration around her schedule. This meant we celebrated on a different day each year, but it was always one day during that week.

Because I was the only one young enough for candles indicating age, I was the only one to blow out the candles on the cake.

At least that's the way it was until Mary's daughter, Chris, came along. When I was turning thirteen and Chris was about four years old, the tradition changed. Chris insisted that everyone should have their own birthday cake. So, all of a sudden, instead of having one cake for three people, we started having three cakes in one week.

By then, Mary and Chris lived just down the street from us, so we were able to have our own cakes on our actual birthdays. We also changed from getting the cakes from the bakery. We started buying them at the grocery store or making them from a mix. Whichever we did, we bought candy decorations to write "Happy Birthday" on the cakes.

The tradition ended when we celebrated with my Dad for the last time, five months before he died. That same year, my sister decided to start celebrating her birthday at home with just her daughter and grandchildren. We had separate cakes for just me and my Dad. I was getting too old for the number of candles required to indicate my age. We decided to use number candles. We used the same two numbers for both my cake and my Dad's, because my age and his were exactly reversed that year. I was twenty-seven and he was seventy-two.

After that, I celebrated my birthday with just my Mom and my brother, Charlie, until my Mom died in 1998— ten years after my Dad died. Then I just celebrated with Charlie until he went into a nursing home. At that time, I moved to a place where several of my friends lived. From then on, I celebrated my birthday with them, some of whom also had September birthdays.

On my fifty-fourth birthday, the last birthday I had during Charlie's lifetime, I decided I wanted to spend my birthday with him. I did not know at the time that it would be the last time I would share my birthday with him. I just knew I wanted to be with my best friend on my birthday that year. I made arrangements with the bus to take me to see him and bring me back home afterwards.

I only got to be with him for a little over an hour, but seeing him was my birthday present to myself. What I didn't know, was that I was also going to get a birthday present from him too. He asked me if I still collected stuffed animals, and I said "Yes". He told me to pick out one from his collection. I chose a big stuffed tiger. That tiger is even more special to me now because it was my last birthday present from Charlie.

Birthday Cake

Ingredients:
- Your wallet with money
- 1 box of cake mix (and the ingredients it requires)
- Candy letters
- 1 can of icing

Directions:

Take your wallet with money in it. Drive, ride your bike, or walk to your nearest grocery store. Once you get to the store, choose your favorite cake mix. Check the directions on the box and make sure you either have at home or buy the things necessary to make the cake from the mix. Then choose your favorite canned icing and get candy letters. Pay for the items. Return home.

Follow directions on cake mix. Let the cake cool. Spread the icing on the cake. Follow the directions on the candy. Put the letters on the cake. If you don't have enough letters in the candy for what you want to spell, be creative. Serve the cake.

SPAGHETTI A-PLENTY

By Jenny Breeden

I grew up during the 1960s in a family with six children. With eight of us around the dinner table every evening, Mom was always trying to save money on the grocery bill while still feeding us a wholesome, well-balanced meal. One of those meals, in fact my favorite one, was her spaghetti.

She made the sauce from scratch from an old family recipe, which she had typed up on an index card and taped to the inside of the cabinet door over the coffee pot. The meaty sauce, poured over pasta, and paired with a tossed salad or a vegetable, like green beans, meant there'd be plenty of food to go around the table. That was important, because my two brothers were, as Mom used to say, "growing boys with big appetites."

When we had spaghetti on Sundays, it became special. Mom would make garlic bread, we'd all get to enjoy a few sips of Chianti, and for dessert, there was always something chocolate.

Birthday celebrations with the grandparents invited often included a spaghetti dinner. If it was a milestone birthday, there'd also be aunts, uncles and cousins.

"It's the perfect thing to serve when you've got a lot of mouths to feed." Mom would say.

One of the first milestone birthdays I remember was my oldest sister Patty's thirteenth. It signified her transition from being a child to finally being a teenager; the first in our family. She was allowed to have a separate "friends" party in the basement. She could invite any of her classmates to her party. Her invitation list only contained girls' names, even though she was allowed to include boys.

When Mom asked her why there were no boys on the list, Patty exclaimed, "Oh, no, I don't want any yucky boys at my party!"

Since JoAnn was twelve and I was ten, and we knew most of her friends, we got invited too. Our younger brothers, Dave and John, were automatically excluded, regardless of their ages— it was now a girls-only party. But at ages eight and six, they were too unruly to be invited anywhere. Our baby sister Cathy was only four, so she had to stay upstairs with the boys and the parents.

The party started with snacks and pop, then a spaghetti dinner, of course, and finally chocolate cake and ice cream. Grandma Smith was there to help out with the serving. She had worked for many years as a waitress at some of the more prestigious restaurants in Cincinnati and Covington. She was sure she could handle this small party.

To save a little money on the party and to reduce the amount of clean up, Mom opted for paper plates. She filled them in the kitchen, and Grandma carried them two at a time to the basement. The first trip went fine. But when she started down with the second pair of plates, they started to buckle. The sauce had laid on the plates a little longer and weakened the paper.

Both plates folded over and before she could catch either one, the spaghetti slid off onto the steps. *Ker splat!* What a glorious mess! The look on Grandma's face was the best part. She apologized the entire time she was cleaning up.

"In all my days on the job, I've never lost a single plate of food. Now, I've lost two in one night." She was so flustered.

We learned our lesson. For every party after that, spaghetti was served on real plates. "Better to do a few more dishes than to have another disaster on our hands." Mom said cheerfully.

When I got older, I copied her recipe onto my own index card. In whatever dorm room, apartment or house I was living in a the time, I taped the index card to the inside of a kitchen cabinet door. I used it to make spaghetti sauce for myself, and later, for my husband and daughter.

For my mother's birthday one year, I got the bright idea to make lasagna instead of spaghetti, but I still used her sauce recipe as the basis for it, ladling it between the layers of pasta and cheeses. Everyone raved over it, and suddenly it became the new birthday meal.

Over the years, in an attempt to make it a healthier, I've modified a few of the ingredients. I've used ground turkey in place of some or all of the beef, used salt-free tomato paste, eliminated the sugar or used calorie-free sugar substitutes, and swapped out the regular pastas for the whole wheat varieties. It is a great recipe for trying out your own substitutions and turning it into your new favorite.

Pat's Perfect Spaghetti Sauce

Ingredients:
- 2 pounds of lean ground beef
- 1 large white onion, finely chopped
- 1 12-ounce can tomato paste
- 3 cups water
- 1 tablespoon grated Parmesan cheese
- 1 tablespoon sugar (reduces the acidity in the tomatoes)
- 1 teaspoon Italian herb seasoning (basil, marjoram, oregano, rosemary, thyme)
- ½ teaspoon salt
- ½ teaspoon garlic powder
- $^1/_8$ teaspoon black pepper

Directions:
Crumble ground beef in a skillet, add chopped onion and fry, stirring and breaking the beef into smaller pieces until thoroughly browned. Drain the beef mixture to remove as much grease as possible. Combine the beef mixture and all other ingredients in a large sauce pan. Cover. Simmer over medium heat for at least twenty

minutes, stirring occasionally to prevent it from sticking to the bottom of the pan and burning. Serve over cooked pasta or rice. Serves 4-6

White Buttercream Icing for Cake and for Decorating

Ingredients:
- ½ cup white solid vegetable shortening
- ½ cup butter or margarine
- 1 teaspoon clear vanilla extract
- 4 cups sifted white confectioners' sugar
- 2 tablespoons milk

Directions:

Mix by hand or with an electric mixer, the shortening and softened (not melted) butter or margarine in a medium bowl. Mix in the vanilla extract. Gradually add the sugar, about a half cup to a cup at a time, mixing thoroughly each time. Slowly add the milk while mixing at a medium speed until the mixture is fluffy.

If you need the mixture thinner for easier spreading, add up to two tablespoons of extra milk, water or light corn syrup. Add extra liquid in increments, and only add as much as needed to achieve the desired consistency. Icing will have an off-white color and will accommodate food coloring for decorating. However, if you need pure white icing for the cake, substitute an additional half cup of white shortening for the butter and add a half teaspoon of clear (no-color) butter flavor.

Mom's Coffee Chocolate Icing

Ingredients:

- 2 ¾ cups white confectioners sugar
- 1 ¼ cups powdered cocoa
- 2 tablespoons cold black coffee

Directions:

Sift together sugar, cocoa, and coffee. For a more robust chocolate flavor, increase the ratio of cocoa to sugar or stir a tablespoon of chocolate syrup into the coffee before adding it to the shortening, butter, sugar and cocoa mixture. Chocolate syrup can also be drizzled over the edges of the cake after it is iced to give it a decorative touch.

2 – SUMMER

BLACKBERRY PICKIN'

By Jenny Breeden

When I was very young, until I was eight years old, my family lived on Hulbert Avenue in Erlanger, Kentucky. At the time, the street dead-ended at a huge wooded area. It was about seven houses past our house. My older sisters and I played in those woods during the summers.

We'd pick wildflowers and bring them home to Mom. She'd put the white and yellow daisies, the blue dandelions or whatever we'd bring her, into a vase in the middle of the kitchen table. We'd admire them while we ate dinner as a family every evening. I guess she didn't have the heart to tell us that most of the "flowers" we brought her were actually weeds but they were so colorful and it was the thought that counted most of all.

We'd play tag with some of the neighbor kids that were our ages. We built forts and hide-outs, using scrap wood and old bed sheets. We'd play 'Cops and Robbers', 'Cowboys and Indians' or some other fantasy storyline one of us dreamed up. Some days, we'd head out for the woods in the morning, just after breakfast and we'd be gone for the whole day. We'd leave when the church bells rang at five minutes before six p.m.— our signal to get home in time for dinner.

In late June through early July, we'd go to the woods with our galvanized buckets to work before we could play. Our "job" was to pick as many blackberries as we could find and haul them home in our buckets. Of course, it wasn't hard finding them; they were everywhere in the woods. However, the tricky part was getting close enough to pick them.

They grew in huge bramble bushes sprawling through the

underbrush. The bushes had long, pointy thorns. When you got to close to them, they stuck you in the fingers, hands, arms or legs. *Not pleasant!* The three of us weren't very tall, so the upper half of any bush was inaccessible. None of us dared to stand on tippy toes and lean into a bush to pick berries. One wrong move, and you'd topple into the bush. Before you could get back on your feet, you'd be scraped up something awful!

Another problem was competition. The ripe berries that were low hanging, the ones easiest for us to pick, were usually eaten by the critters running loose in the woods— squirrels, rabbits, raccoons and opossums, to name just a few. Occasionally, we'd see one of these hungry critters still eating in the bramble bush. I don't know which was more scared, the poor defenseless animal or us three sisters.

We had to be careful not to fill the buckets so full we couldn't carry them. If the bucket was a little too heavy, we'd pick through the berries, looking for the juiciest ones to eat, to lighten the load. We'd already picked them so we couldn't just throw them out.

"They'll make it home one way or another." One of us would say, as we'd each stuff a handful of berries in our mouths.

Once we got home, Mom would thank each one of us as she dumped our bucket into the kitchen sink and washed the berries with cold water. Then she would divide them into three batches. One batch was for eating over our cereal in the mornings. She'd just drain the water off those berries, put them into a Tupperware bowl with a lid and pop them into the fridge to get cold.

Another batch she'd drain and pat dry. She'd put them into a large freezer bag and lay the bag flat, squeezing out all the air before sealing it. She'd place them flat on the shelf in the freezer and say, "See you this winter, my sweet little things."

Now came the best part. The last batch was for a blackberry cobbler, our dessert for after dinner. I would watch her as she'd dig out all the ingredients and prepare the baking dish.

"You know what, Mom?" I had asked her on one occasion as she was stirring the hot berry mixture on the stove.

"Know what, honey?"

"This is my favorite part of the whole blackberry pickin' experience," I had replied, smiling up at her. "Watching you fix cobbler and knowing I'll get to eat some right after dinner tonight."

The warm cobbler with a small dollop of vanilla ice cream on top made the close encounters with Mother Nature's scavengers, the thorn stabbings, scrapes and scratches, and even the little blisters on my hands from hauling the heavy bucket back home all worth it.

When I was eight, my parents moved us to the other side of Erlanger. That house was bigger, but it was on a street with lots of houses and no woods nearby. At least no woods with blackberries. When school let out for the summer, my sisters and I hopped on our Schwinn banana seat bicycles and peddled all the way across town to the end of Hulbert Avenue, to our beloved woods and our blackberry patch.

We had wicker baskets, lined with double-bagged paper grocery bags, strapped in front of the handle bars. We loaded them with as many blackberries as we could get in them. Each summer, we did the berry runs as often as we could, until there were no more ripe berries to pick.

We continued our traditional summer visits to our blackberry woods for a few years. Then, one day we rode up, baskets lined with paper bags, ready to do some berry pickin' only to find bulldozers and other construction equipment in the same spot where the woods and bramble bushes had been. Apparently the city had decided Hulbert Avenue could be extended and eventually linked up with another road leading into Crescent Springs. Our woods had to go in the name of progress.

Whenever I eat a bowlful of blackberry cobbler with a little vanilla ice cream, I'm eight years old and back in the woods again, playing in my hideout with my sisters and loving every minute of it.

Blackberry Cobbler

Filling Ingredients:
- 3 cups fresh (or frozen) blackberries
- 1 cup sugar
- 3 tablespoons cornstarch
- 1 cup cold water
- 1 tablespoon butter (or margarine)

Biscuit Topping Ingredients:
- 1 ½ cups all-purpose flour
- 1 tablespoon sugar
- 1 ½ teaspoons baking powder
- ½ teaspoon salt
- ½ cup cold butter, cubed
- ½ cup milk (2% or whole)

Directions:

If you want to make this recipe faster, you can use Bisquick biscuit mix and follow the package directions to make the batter. You can also use a can of prepared regular buttermilk biscuits. Just chop them up into smaller pieces and place them on top of the berry mixture.

Whipped topping or vanilla ice cream is optional (but I can't imagine warm cobbler without a cream topping of some sort.)

In a large saucepan, combine the blackberries and one cup of sugar. Cook and stir until the mixture comes to a boil. Combine the cornstarch and water until smooth; stir into the fruit mixture. Return to a boil, cooking and stirring for an additional two minutes or until thickened. Pour into a greased eight-inch square backing pan (glass or metal). Dot with butter on top.

For the biscuit topping, in a small mixing bowl, combine the flour, sugar, baking powder and salt. Cut in the butter cubes until the mixture is coarse crumbs. Stir in the milk until just moistened. Scoop out with tablespoon and drop onto the hot berry mixture.

Bake at 350° F uncovered for thirty to thirty-five minutes or until berry filling is bubbling and the biscuit topping is a light golden brown. Serve warm, with the topping if desired.

Makes about 9 servings.

FOURTH OF JULY FIREWORKS

By Mikey Chlanda

Each year, at Dave's insistence, the Fire Department participated in the Fairborn July Fourth Parade. It was traditional to throw penny candies from the rigs at the little kids sitting along parade route hoping to catch them. Concerned about any remote potential for liability, Fairborn officially looked down on candy-throwing, but they turned a blind eye on it in practice.

The first year we were in the parade, Dave and I threw candy from the top of number 702, the Clifton tanker/pumper. Dave, at this point in his life, was a die-hard single guy, hitting on most women he saw. During the parade, he pointed out some woman in the crowd along the route.

"She's hot!"

I looked to see who he was pointing at. I cracked up. It was Ruthanne, a good friend of mine. I elbowed Dave. "Watch this."

"Hey babe. You are smoking hot!"

Even though I was in my gear, Ruthanne recognized me and laughed. "You're smoking hot yourself, MIS-TER FI-RE-MAN!"

"Wanna go out with me?"

"Sure. When?"

"Tonight, six p.m. at HaHa's in Yellow Springs."

"You're on! Meet you there."

Dave was speechless.

I was nonchalant and just played it off, saying, "That's how you do it, Dave."

He just shook his head in amazement. When we got back to the firehouse, he was still flabbergasted. He told everyone how I had asked out some smoking hot blonde chick at the parade. "You should'a seen him. He just shouted at her from the top of the rig and had a date in a thirty second conversation."

When I got home, I had a message from Ruthanne on my answering machine.

"It's Ruthanne. I just want you to know that you are really buying me dinner tonight at HaHa's at six p.m. for playing along with your stupid firefighter joke."

I just want you to know, Ruthanne, it was worth every penny for that dinner. Possibly triple.

A year later, we rode in the parade again. By this time, Dave was dating Steph (his future wife). He was driving the rig, and Steph and I were on top, throwing candy to the kiddies. Along the parade route, we passed a few middle-aged guys sitting in lawn chairs. They saw Steph and started hooting and whistling at her.

One yelled, "Hey baby, you can give me mouth to mouth anytime."

Even though we both knew he was yelling at Steph, I yelled back without hesitation. "Hey baby yourself. I'm the only paramedic on this rig. You want mouth to mouth, I'll give it to you right here, right now."

The guy turned beet red. Even better, his friends turned on him, giving him shit for asking another guy to give him mouth to mouth.

Steph was still embarrassed from being harassed, but she turned to me and gave a squeeze to my shoulder. "Mikey, you are such a dick sometimes with your smart-ass mouth, but right now I love you. I was too shocked to say anything back to him."

"No worries, Steph. I got your back."

Red, White and Blue Cookout

Cook hamburgers, hotdogs and other meats on a grill.
Enjoy these vegetables: sliced red tomatoes, fresh or slightly grilled, and red bell pepper strips, fresh or grilled.

Slice white onions and separate into rings. Place them in a bowl of cold water, colored blue with all natural food coloring until they start to absorb the color. Drain and place on a serving plate.

As an alternate, take a slice of tomato, a slice of white onion and some bleu cheese to make a Red, White and Bleu burger.

JULY FOURTH

By Jenny Breeden

Sweat beads from my ice cold can of pop
Drip on my bare feet, tickling my toes.
Oh, how I love a hot summer day!

Cardinals chatter up in the trees.
Old Glory flutters as the breeze blows.
Oh, how I love a hot summer day!

Sweet smell of fresh cut grass fills the air
From the neighbor's front yard as he mows.
Oh, how I love a hot summer day!

Children play baseball out in the street.
Batter steps to the plate, pitcher throws.
Oh, how I love a hot summer day!

Savor a treat of marshmallow s'mores.
Relaxing while the bonfire glows.
Oh, how I love a cool summer night!

I've always enjoyed our family picnic or cookouts on July Fourth. To make the day fun while we waited for the food to cook or for it to get dark enough to shoot off fireworks, I supplied food and craft projects for anyone interested in creating them. Here are a few of my favorites.

Patriotic Pins

Supplies:

- 2 ¼ inch coil-less safety pins (can be purchased at a fabric/sewing store, craft store or online, 50 pins cost about $4.00, can be stainless steel, nickel, silver tone, gold tone, copper tone)
- Four medium sized beads in each color - Red, White and Blue plastic beads, acrylic or opaque (the center hole should not be much larger than the pin thickness)
- Patriotic ribbon, cut in 2 ½ inch pieces
- Metal crimping beads, color should match the safety pins (stainless steel, nickel, silver tone, gold tone, copper tone)
- Pliers

Instructions:

Take one safety pin and open it. Slide six beads onto the pin in alternating colors, red, white, blue, red, white, blue to the pin head. Take the strip of ribbon and loop it at the top and cross it over in the middle. Holding it together, slide the pin point through the double-thickness at the middle of the ribbon, from the underneath on the one side over the top of the ribbon and then down through the other side. Position the ribbon against the last blue bead. Slide the remaining beads onto the pin next to the ribbon in reverse order, blue, white, red, blue, white, red. Do not push them too tight against the ribbon.

The beads and ribbon combination should cover the top part of the pin and end at the curved part of the pin. Take one crimping bead and slide it onto the pin and position it next to last red bead. Using the pliers, squeeze the crimping bead together tightly. This should keep all the beads from sliding back around the curve into the "pin" side. Attach the pin to a collar, shirt pocket, purse strap or where ever you like to show you pride in the USA.

Foam Picture Frames

Supplies:

- 9x12 inch, 2 mm thick foam sheets in red, white and blue colors
- 1 roll of ¼ inch double-sided tape
- Assorted patriotic foam shapes, (flags, fireworks, stars, etc.), self-adhesive if you can find them
- Assorted color fine point Sharpie pens
- Adhesive magnet strip, cut into 1 inch pieces
- Sharp knife or box cutter
- Pencil
- Ruler

Instructions:

In advance of July Fourth, an adult should take the 9x12 inch foam sheets, ruler, pencil and cutting tool. Measure six inches from the edge to the center of the 12-inch side of the foam sheet. Mark the line with the pencil and cut the foam sheet on the line, using the edge of the ruler as a guide to keep the cut straight. Take one half of each sheet and set them aside. These will be the backs of the frames. Take the other half of each sheet and determine which side will be the back.

On the back, measure 1 inch from each edge into the middle and mark it with the pencil. Put at least two marks on each side. Using the ruler, line up the marks and make lines around the interior, connecting them at each corner. With the cutting tool, carefully cut along the lines, using the edge of the ruler as your guide. Be careful not to cut too far into the corners. When the entire rectangular area has been cut, pop the center piece of foam out of the middle. These are the fronts of the frames.

Note: If you want to make smaller frames out of the middles, take half of the pieces and set them aside for the backs. Take the other halves and follow the same steps as above except measure ¾ inch in from each edge.

On July Fourth, party guests can take a frame back and pair it with a frame front. Turn the frame front over and put double sided tape on the bottom and two sides only. Remove the tape protector and press the frame front to the back, ensuring the edge without tape is at the top of the frame. This will allow you to slide a picture into the frame without worrying it will slide out the bottom. With the frame back and front securely attached, decorate the front of the frame with the foam shapes and use the Sharpie pens to write on the frames and shapes.

You can write "July 4th" and the year. "Happy Birthday, USA", your family name with "Cookout" or "Picnic", or anything else you want to write. Take two pieces of magnetic strip and put one on the left side and the other on the right side of the back of the frame. Insert your favorite picture of the day and put the frame on the refrigerator or other metal surface.

Patriotic Cupcakes

Supplies:
- 1 box cake mix (your favorite kind) and the required ingredients to make the mix
- Cupcake papers
- 1 or more cans of white frosting
- Red, white and blue sprinkles
- Red, white and blue candies
- Red and blue tubes of decorating frosting
- American Flag cupcake picks

- Paper plates
- Butter knives

Instructions:

Bake cupcakes the day before or the early afternoon of the Fourth, using your favorite recipe or box mix. Pour into cupcake papers in a cupcake baking pan. Bake according to the recipe or box instructions. Cool before decorating.

After the dinner has been cleaned up, set up the table with cupcakes, frosting, paper plates, butter knives, and decorating supplies. Each person gets to frost and decorate their own cupcakes, show them off to the other party guests and enjoy them while they wait for the fireworks show to being.

3 – FALL

COLD DAY – WARM SOUP

By Elle Mott

My life is simple, sometimes out of circumstance; usually because that's how I like it. I don't tweet what I think of you or add you as my friend on Facebook. Instead, I call you from my phone and tell you why I like you. I don't have a dog to walk each morning. I have pet finches who sing good morning to me. Playtime is absent of children of my own but I smile at the spark of curiosity in each child I see in passing as they look to their adult companion for answers.

I don't have to drive everywhere I go. When I walk the few blocks to the neighborhood grocery store I'm able to see the latest blooms on your rose bushes or stop to share a hello with you. At the grocery store, I needn't be impatient to get through the line. The more time I have next to you in our wait, the more moments we have to introduce ourselves and to openly share one good thought. I don't watch the latest show on primetime TV. Instead, I read the next chapter in a compelling historical novel or better yet, write the next chapter in my book of life.

Special occasions, from birthdays to New Year's Eve champagne parties to Fourth of July firework displays can find me most anywhere and open to endless possibilities. Relishing my friendship bonds are the one constant I keep as days become holidays. And as the warmer days melt away into the colder season, my friends and neighbors are likely planning their next big holiday family gathering. Whereas, I traditionally look forward to the first cold day because it is my time to let go of the hustle and bustle of spring and summer activities to rediscover comfort and warmth in my home.

On the first cold day following the warm season —and this

might not correlate to any designated day on our calendar— I traditionally cook up a full pot of a homemade vegetable soup. I then settle in to my favorite pastime, which for me is to write creatively while watching over my pet finches build winter nests together in their aviary. I give you my soup recipe so you too may give yourself a day to enjoy at your favorite in-home pastime, whether it be writing or reading or maybe a jigsaw puzzle or even a handicraft project.

<u>Warm Soup Recipe</u>

Ingredients:
- 1 Pound ground beef, 80% or more lean
- Dried basil (a few pinches, to taste)
- Dried oregano (a few pinches, to taste)
- Ground black pepper (a few pinches, to taste)
- Seasoning salt (a few pinches, to taste)
- Dried thyme (a few pinches, to taste)
- 2 eggs (white or brown)
- Crackers (about ½ package)
- 1 16-ounce bag of fresh baby carrots
- 1 celery stalk
- 1 head of broccoli
- 1 head of cauliflower
- 1 can whole yellow kernel corn (about 15 ounces)
- 1 can whole green peas (about 15 ounces)
- 2 cans whole stewed Italian tomatoes
- 2 big bay leaves, dried
- 10 whole white mushrooms
- 6 large russet brown potatoes

Directions:

First, mix the ground beef, basil, oregano, pepper, seasoning salt, thyme, eggs, and crackers into a firm consistency. Then, pinching a little mixture at a time, use your hands to roll into meatballs. I then nuke these meatballs for about five minutes. Alternatively, you can fry on the stove. Cook until about medium rare. (Don't worry, they'll cook up more later.) Drain and set aside.

Next, put a tall soup pot on the stove top burner. My pot is fourteen inches high with a ten-inch diameter. Add water about one-third up. Turn on the heat to a high simmer.

Add the carrots. Cut the celery to about the same length as the carrots, but keep fat. Add these. Cut the flowers off the stems of the broccoli and cut the cauliflower into large bite-sized pieces, discarding the hard stems. Keep in mind, the cauliflower will crumble as it cooks. Add the cauliflower, and then the broccoli. All thus far should simmer at just below the water line for about ten minutes. If needed, add a little water, just enough to cover everything.

Add the meatballs. Add corn, peas, and tomatoes, liquid included (do not drain any of the canned items). Stir gently. Drop in the bay leaves. Continue to let the pot simmer. Do not let it boil.

Cut the mushrooms in quarters and do the same with the potatoes. Add the mushrooms but set aside the potatoes. Let simmer about another twenty minutes. Add the potatoes and let simmer about another thirty minutes.

Lastly, with a dipping ladle, serve yourself a deep bowl of the savory soup. Keep the pot of soup on warm to help yourself to seconds and thirds or to nibble on all day. Enjoy as you enjoy your first cold day on the home-front.

FALL FESTIVAL FUN

By Brad Hudepohl

Every year, on the first Sunday in October, my family traveled from Cincinnati, Ohio to Oldenburg, Indiana for the Holy Family Catholic Church Festival. My aunts, uncles, cousins, and my Mom and Dad attended. I am not sure how the tradition started; perhaps it was because my Uncle Bud owned a farm about thirty miles away, outside of Greensburg, Indiana. A distinguishing fact about Greensburg is the tree which grows out of the courthouse tower.

Holy Family had a typical festival with bingo, cards, and the selling of chances at various booths to win hams, turkeys, toys, gift baskets, quilts, afghans, and more. The best part was the food, which was served in the school's cafeteria, directly below its gymnasium. They served turkey, roast beef, mashed potatoes, green beans, corn, coleslaw, applesauce; and my favorite, fresh tomatoes.

Stuffed with food, we next visited the different booths in the gymnasium and outside in the schoolyard. One booth had a loud machine which spat and sputtered and frightened me when I was a small child. It made ice cream —the best ice cream I have ever eaten! Another booth sold mock turtle soup (my Dad's favorite.) My Mom and Dad always bought the soup, but if the booth sold out, Mom would make some at home.

After Holy Family's festival, we would visit my Uncle Bud's farm outside of Greensburg. The farm had a barn, cornfield, lake, a large unfarmed area, and a small white board house. That house had a sink in the kitchen with a hand operated water pump and also a well in its front yard. My cousins and I played in the cornfield, staying clear of the mama pig that became quite angry if we went near her piglets. A bull was fenced in next to the barn with an old tractor and car inside.

Once, my Dad, uncle, and cousins brought fishing gear to the farm. When we went down a hill on our way to fish at the lake, several cows ran after us. We quickly hid behind some trees as they stampeded by. I do not remember if we caught fish that day.

Mom, Dad, my aunts, and uncles have passed on, but I have continued our tradition. I cherish this family tradition and I am thankful they gave it to me.

Mock Snapped Turtle Soup

Ingredients:
- 2 ½ pounds cut-up sirloin
- 8 tablespoons butter
- 2 stalks of cut-up celery
- 1 cut-up green pepper
- 1 cut-up onion
- 4 minced garlic cloves
- 1 can (about 18 ounces) crushed or stewed tomatoes
- 6 cups water
- Beef Broth (about 30 ounces)
- 1 cup flour and water paste
- 3 tablespoons Worcestershire Sauce
- ¾ cup catsup
- Pinch of salt
- Pinch of black pepper
- 1 teaspoon thyme
- 1 tablespoon paprika
- ½ teaspoon cayenne
- 1 ½ cup lemon juice
- 4 hardboiled chopped eggs

Directions:

Cook sirloin in frying pan with butter, celery, green pepper, onion, and garlic. Transfer to a large pot. Add tomatoes, water, beef broth, flour paste, Worcestershire Sauce, catsup, salt, black pepper, thyme, paprika, cayenne, and lemon juice. Cook on medium heat for three to four hours. Reduce heat to a simmer. Add eggs. Serve warm.

HALLOWEEN CHILI

By Jenny Breeden

The weather in October in the Ohio River Valley is unpredictable, to say the least. There have been days in the mid-80s when you see people wearing t-shirts and shorts and also some days in the mid-40s when people are breaking out their winter coats and gloves. The overnight lows can range from the 50s to the low 30s.

In my lifetime, I've seen tornado warnings, high winds, and the remnants of hurricanes during October. I've also seen frost warnings, hard freezes and even snow events. By the time we get to the end of the month, there's no telling what the daytime temperature will be or how quickly the temperature will drop during the two-hour span for Trick-or-Treating.

The unpredictability of the weather makes picking out a Halloween costume challenging. Each year, when my daughter, Elizabeth, was young, I tried to help her decide what she wanted to dress up as. It always came down to what we thought the weather would be on that night. There was nothing worse than having the most adorable costume completely hidden under a winter coat, hat and mittens.

In 1993, we worked very hard to create the perfect costume – Michelangelo. No, not the famous Italian master of the Renaissance, the teenage mutant ninja turtle with the jovial attitude from the New York City sewer system. We were ready a week in advance and Elizabeth was so excited to show it off to all the neighbors and everyone else.

It started snowing in the evening of October 30 and continued to snow overnight. By the time it finished the next morning, Covington had four and a half inches on the ground. Many of the outlying areas of Greater Cincinnati had about six inches. Most of these areas canceled Trick-or-Treating or postponed it for a couple of days. Covington held its on Halloween night as originally planned and Junior took Elizabeth around to just the closest neighbors. She had to hold the turtle shell because it wouldn't fit under her winter coat nor would it go on over it. By the time Halloween rolled around the next year, the turtle costume didn't fit, and we had to come up with another one.

Another challenging aspect of Trick-or-Treating was time schedule. It started at six p.m. and ended at eight. I left work in Cincinnati at five p.m., fought traffic across the river to the sitters' house to get Elizabeth, and drove past the in-laws' to pick up Junior. That meant we were lucky to pull up in front of our house by six. We dashed inside, he helped her into the costume and I grabbed the candy bags just about at the same time the doorbell was announcing the arrival of the first set of treaters at the door.

Junior took the little princess, wicked witch, Dalmatian puppy or whatever she was dressed up to be that year while I sat on the porch, passing out candy to assorted gremlins, fairies, zombies and superheroes. It seemed like no time at all, it was eight o'clock and the event was over and we were faced with another challenge, what to eat for dinner.

"I want pizza, Mommy!"

"Why don't you just run out and pick up burgers and fries," Junior suggested. Seeing the frown on my face, he added "It will be faster than fixing something here."

"I guess you're right. Even if I start something now, it will be almost nine before we start eating." While sitting in the drive-thru along with many other parents who made the same "easy" dinner decision, I thought there had to be a better way. "Next year, I'm going to plan ahead," I said to myself, and a new Halloween tradition was started.

On the morning of October 31, I got up a little early, took twenty minutes to prepare my favorite chili recipe and throw it all into the crockpot. I plugged it in, switched it on Low, set the timer for seven hours and finished getting ready for work.

By the time we got home, it was ready. I could smell it as soon as I opened the front door. I fixed a small bowl of chili with some shredded cheese for each of us, and we ate it after we finished getting the costume on and the candy bowl ready. A few bites was enough to keep us satisfied until eight o'clock when Trick-or-Treat time was over.

Then, we got another bowl full with spaghetti and crackers and maybe a Coney Island to go with it. We sat down around the kitchen table and had a family dinner while we talked about the various costumes we'd seen and all the candy Elizabeth got in her bag.

As Elizabeth got older and she developed friendships with a few of the neighborhood girls, we'd invite them and their parents to our house for chili and coneys. There's nothing better than relaxing with family and friends over a nice warm bowl of chili, especially on a chilly Halloween night.

Crockpot Chili

Ingredients:

- 2 pounds lean (at least 80%) ground beef (or 1 pound beef and 1 pound ground turkey)
- 1 finely chopped large white onion
- 2 cans (14 ½ ounces each) undrained diced tomatoes
- 1 can (15 ounces) drained and rinsed light red kidney beans (I prefer to use Joan of Arc brand beans)
- 1 can (15 ounces) Joan of Arc Spicy Chili Beans
- 1 can (15 ½ ounces) tomato sauce
- 2 tablespoon chili powder
- 1 tablespoons dried oregano
- 1 tablespoon cocoa powder

- 1 ½ teaspoon ground cumin
- 1 teaspoon garlic powder
- ½ teaspoon salt
- ½ teaspoon black pepper
- ¼ teaspoon cayenne pepper

Optional:

- Shredded cheese (American or mild cheddar)
- Oyster (Soup & Chili) Crackers or regular saltine crackers
- Cooked spaghetti (prepared per package instructions) or cooked rice as an alternative

Coney Islands:

- Hot dogs and buns
- Yellow mustard
- Diced white onions

Directions:

Brown ground beef (and turkey if desired) and chopped onions in a large skillet on the stove over medium-high heat until meat is all brown and onions are transparent. Drain fat and place meat mixture in the bottom of a crockpot or slow cooker.

Put the remaining ingredients and seasonings in the crockpot and stir to mix them thoroughly. Cook for seven to eight hours on LOW or four hours on HIGH, stirring occasionally. Serves many, especially if you add the additional items previously mentioned.

Optional step:

After you brown and drain the meat and onions but before you add in all the other ingredients to the crock pot, put the can of red kidney beans, drained and rinsed, and up to half the can of the spicy chili beans with the sauce into a blender. Blend until the beans and shells are pureed. Add in about half a can of diced tomatoes and blend again to thoroughly mix together. Pour the pureed bean/tomato mixture into the crockpot over the cooked meat/onions.

NOTE: This is a step I had to add because my daughter, about five years old at the time, was a very picky eater. Although I tried to get her to eat beans for the health benefits, she did not like them in her chili. She would pick out every single bean she could find and put them on her plate. This process took a long time, and it drove me crazy. She'd whine and complain the whole time, and I had to throw the beans in the garbage, wasting them. With the majority of the beans pulverized beyond recognition, it took her less time to pick through her chili to find "all" the beans in her bowl, about ten at most, which made everyone was a lot happier.

"Hey, Mom, did you do something different with the chili?" she had asked that first time, as she stirred through her bowl, picking out another bean. "I can't find as many beans as I normally do."

"I'm happy you noticed," I replied. "I got tired of you spending so much time picking them out, so I decided to change up the recipe so you wouldn't have to deal with so many whole beans in your bowl."

"Great, thanks Mom!" She smiled. "I'm already finished finding them all," she announced. She ate a huge spoonful. "Yum...it still tastes as good as it ever did."

She was right! It still tasted like it always did. In fact, I noticed that I too enjoyed having fewer visible beans, especially on my coneys. I never told her my secret process, so she never knew she was eating beans in her chili.

"MOON BLESSED" APPLE BUTTER: A FAMILY TRADITION

By Ginny Shephard

Aunt Bess had a rule: meet at her place on the Saturday nearest the full moon *after* Johnny Appleseed's September 26 birthday for our family Apple Festival. She figured by mid-October the nearby orchard's supply of McIntosh apples, her favorite, would be plump and juicy. Then all the aunts, uncles, cousins, and any neighbors Aunt Bess and Uncle Ollie could grab would make "moon-blessed" apple butter.

We kids were wretchedly back in school by then, but this time of stirring the big copper pot was the most fun we'd have until Halloween. We hoped to be deemed "big enough this year" to help the adults turn apples into that spicy nut-brown butter.

It took all day. Uncle Ollie would have already cut and stacked the hardwood from his woods behind their white farmhouse with the huge porch off the kitchen. I always wanted to get there early enough to help him lay the fire. We kids would pester him to let us make the teepee of tinder and set it on fire, and then add the cut logs "with plenty of space for the air, now!"

When it got just right, he'd yell to Aunt Bess, "Let's get on with it."

She had already prepared tons of apples, cooking and mushing them into applesauce, and collected all the spices and whatnot. Above all, she made certain never to let anyone else wash and sterilize all the Mason jars and lids.

Thank goodness! We had enough of that when Mom canned tomatoes.

Between calls to "watch the fire" and "keep stirring now; you don't want it to burn," we kids teased, whispered secrets, and listened to the "old folks" gossip. I loved to watch the gold sauce boil in the sweet cider. The men pulled from a jug of hard cider, "just to wet our whistles," Daddy said.

Finally, it was time to add sugar and then the cinnamon, cloves, and a skoosh of nutmeg —Uncle Ollie's request.

Then the stirring got big-time serious. Big brown bubbles rose and popped, shooting out spiced air. We kids always got shooed away from the boiling goodness, so we swooped back and forth on the tire swings hanging from trees out by the tool shed or played tag. Soon we'd make our way to the kitchen and helped ourselves to heaps of food laid by to feed all the kettle tenders. Beyond the usual macaroni, potato, and Jell-O salads, all the aunts provided their best apple treats: pies, dumplings, and fritters. Aunt Bess supplied the fresh cream.

We younger girls looked forward to the time when Aunt Bess and Uncle Ollie's girls, both in high school, would invite us to join their special corner on the porch. They were always giggling—they dated boys! When we got too near, they shot us "booger-eye" looks.

The big moment came, confirmed by the other Moms, when Aunt Bess declared, "Time to fill the jars, girls!"

Of course she had baked bread and biscuits to sop up all the left over apple butter. Warm bread and melting sweet cream butter, topped with apple butter: enough to make your tongue roll out and shout "Hallelujah!"

Basic Apple Butter

Ingredients:

- One half bushel or approx. 64 medium, nicely flavored cooking apples of your choice.
- 1-gallon sweet cider
- 12 cups sugar (or 6 cups packed brown sugar, according to taste)

- 2 tablespoons cinnamon (or to taste)
- ½ tablespoon ground cloves
- Depending on your taste, could add ½ teaspoon allspice and/or nutmeg

Directions:

Wash and "CCC": Core, Cut, and Cook the apples with sweet cider until you can mash them into applesauce. Stir often. Strain the applesauce in a sieve.

Add sugar, cinnamon, and cloves. Cook outside in an iron or copper kettle or inside in a large stock pot, three or more hours. Stir often. Seal in sterilized jars.

Should fill about twelve to fifteen pints.

4 – THANKSGIVING

FIREHOUSE THANKSGIVING

By Mikey Chlanda

Our Thanksgiving Day tradition on the fire department started back in the late '80s after Dave joined. I usually volunteered to take shifts on the big holidays, like Thanksgiving and Christmas, because I was single and didn't have family in the area. Like me, Dave was single. He suggested we have a mini-Thanksgiving feast at the firehouse for all the other singles on the department who didn't have family plans for the day.

The first year, there were only three or four of us. I roasted a duck, stuffed it with a sausage dressing (my family favorite), and added dumplings and gravy. Dave made a salad and brought some beverages. We turned on the football game in the day room and angled it towards the kitchen, so we could follow the Lions game.

Dinner was early afternoon. Luckily, there were no runs during the day so we got to eat our meal uninterrupted – a rare occurrence at our station. We had a few more people stop by later in the day. It was a nice way to get your holiday greetings in on the appropriate day and chat with some brothers you wouldn't normally get to see.

Probably a dozen people showed up the next year. We moved on up from just one duck to making a few of them and a Cornish hen. We had a sign-up sheet for people to bring sides so we wouldn't wind up with forty-eight servings of mashed potatoes and no desserts.

Dave's girlfriend, Steph (who was also on the fire department roster) stopped by later in the afternoon to see Dave. When she saw the fast-dwindling spread, she ran home to her parents' house and gathered up all their leftovers to bring back to the firehouse. She had probably heard the old adage, if you ever visit a firehouse, you

NEED to bring food, if you want them to talk to you. Well, it worked and a new tradition was started.

The next year, when firefighters' family dinners started breaking up around three or four in the afternoon, they would bring all their leftovers down to us at the firehouse. Sometimes our second dinner was even bigger than our first.

It petered out after ten or fifteen years, as people got married and had kids, developing their own family traditions or moved out of town. It still brings back fond memories for me.

Awesome Sausage Apple Dressing

Ingredients:

- 5 cups roughly torn bread – French is good, day old French baguettes are perfect, if available. If not, wheat or white bread is fine to use.
- 1 cup finely chopped onion
- 1 pound ground sausage (Bob Evans Mild Country Sausage is recommended or Sage if they don't have plain.) Do not get the Italian sausage or any variety with other strong flavors.
- ¾ cup chopped celery
- 2 ½ teaspoons dried sage
- 1 ½ teaspoons dried rosemary
- ½ teaspoon dried thyme
- 1 Golden Delicious apple (peeled, cored and chopped)
- ¾ to 1 cup chopped dried cranberries
- $^1/_3$ cup minced fresh parsley
- 1 finely chopped cooked turkey liver
- ¼ cup melted butter (unsalted is recommended)
- ¾ cup turkey or chicken stock (I used homemade chicken stock since I always had some on hand at the firehouse)

Directions:

Preheat oven to 350° F (75 ° C). Spread the torn bread pieces in a single layer on a backing sheet. Bake for five to seven minutes, until evenly toasted. Transfer the toasted bread to a large bowl.

In a large skillet, cook the chopped onions and sausage over medium heat, breaking the sausage into small bits as it cooks until it is evenly browned. Add the celery, sage, rosemary and thyme; cook, stirring, for an additional two minutes to blend flavors.

Pour sausage mixture over the toasted bread in the large bowl. Toss gently with large spoon or hands. Mix in the chopped apples, cranberries, parsley and liver. Drizzle with melted butter and stock. Mix lightly until mixture is moist but not wet. Allow mixture to cool completely. Spoon or stuff by hand into turkey to loosely fill the cavity. Cook the turkey according to the "stuffed" directions.

If baking the remaining portion of the dressing or if baking the entire batch of dressing, pre-heat the oven to 350° F. Lightly spray the sides and bottom of a glass baking dish with non-stick spray and pour in the mixture. Add more stock/melted butter to ensure the dressing will stay moist when baking. Bake for thirty to forty-five minutes until lightly browned and crispy on top.

FOREVER THANKFUL

By Jenny Breeden

My holiday tradition started many years ago, when I brought my now famous Braunschweiger dip to my sister's house for our family's Thanksgiving dinner. At the time, I wasn't sure what I was going to bring as my contribution to the meal. The turkey, dressing and all the traditional side dishes had already been assigned to other family members.

"So, what should I bring?" I asked my Sister, Cathy. "What about a desert?"

"There should be plenty," Cathy announced. "Patty's making something with pumpkin in it. And we definitely don't need any more pies. Mom's bringing her famous mince pie, Lil has a regular pumpkin pie and an apple pie, and JoAnn said she's got a chocolate cream pie…'cuz that's all Lynn likes."

"So what does that leave for me?"

"Well, everyone usually starts showing up around three o'clock. It'll still be several hours before dinner's ready. So…what about hors d'oeuvres? Can you bring some snacks? Uh…you know, like chips and salsa or pretzels…for folks to nibble on while we wait?"

"I guess," I replied with disappointment. I figured no one would be interested in snacks because they wouldn't want to risk filling up that close to dinner time. Besides, there was no fun or creativity involved in throwing a bunch of bags into a grocery cart. I wanted to bring something that would highlight my cooking talents.

I decided that if I was bringing snacks, they weren't going to be the "same old same old". I had recently learned how to make Braunschweiger dip that was great on crackers, rye bread pieces or even pretzels. I went to the store a few days before Thanksgiving and got all the ingredients.

On Thanksgiving morning, I whipped up a batch. The house smelled wonderful from the liver sausage and the onion soup mix. I put it in the freezer so it would get good and cold. About two o'clock, I got everything we were taking to Cathy's together and into the car. We drove to Crittenden.

We enjoyed the get-together at my sister's and the dip was a big hit. Nearly everyone who tried the dip loved it. Cathy even begged me to let her keep the leftovers.

She said, "It will make a great sandwich spread for my lunch tomorrow," she laughed and added, "I don't think I'll be in the mood for turkey."

Of course, I obliged her request. After messing with that turkey all morning and cooking it all day, I didn't blame her for not wanting to have anything to with it for a day or two.

Braunschweiger Dip

Ingredients
- 1 pound roll of Braunschweiger
- 1 16 ounce tub of sour cream
- 1 package dry onion soup mix
- 5 splashes Worcestershire sauce

Directions

Take the package of onion soup mix and lay it flat on the counter top, unopened. Take a coffee cup or mug and with the rounded bottom edge, press it against the package to break up the onion pieces into smaller bits. After a few minutes of crushing the soup mix, open and empty the contents into a large mixing bowl. Add the sour cream and stir, making sure the dry soup mix is well mixed in. Add the cut up chunks of the Braunschweiger and the splashes of Worcestershire sauce. Beat together with mixer on low speed at first to break up all the chunks. Advance to high speed to whip the mixture until fluffy. Clean excess dip off the mixer beaters and transfer the dip onto two smaller covered bowls. Put in refrigerator for at least two hours to allow the onions to soften. Serve chilled with crackers, rye bread pieces or pretzels.

WHAT IS BEST ABOUT THANKSGIVING

By Alvena Stanfield

NOTE: Names have been changed to avoid future repercussions from not-so-innocent attendees. –A.S.

Since the city's six p.m. siren, Amy Sutton had opened her door and given candy bars to princesses, angels, Spidermen, Hulks, Schreks, pirates and short cross-dressers. When the nine p.m. siren signaled the end of Trick or Treat, she turned off her zombie-masked porch light. Blackberry wine chilling in the fridge was a treat she looked forward to. Before she could eject a milk jug and wrestle the bottle into her hand, the buzzing doorbell followed by a chorus of "Trick or Treat" sent her hurrying, barefoot to the front door.

Peeking out, she was eye-to-eye with a penguin clutch. The tall, auburn-haired one, accompanied by two shorter auburn-haired penguins, brought an instant smile. She jerked the door open and hugged all three.

"Twick tweet, Auntomy" told her this shortest penguin was four-year-old Emma. Bert, eight, and their mother waddled into Amy's foyer with Emma and they took off their masks.

"Do you like our costumes? I made them myself," Tara said.

"Outstanding, great job." Amy spun the two short penguins around, admiring Tara's handiwork. "How about cookies for little penguins and a blackberry pick-me-up for Mom?"

Amy filled two wine glasses and set a plate on the table piled high with chocolate chip cookies.

Tara sipped her wine, took a deep breath and leaned closer to Amy.

"What about Thanksgiving, Aunt Amy? The best ones are here

at your house." She looked away, studying the wall clock.

Unblinking, Amy stared. For the past three years, she and Joe bore the prep, cost and cleanup.

"Isn't it your mother's turn? Or how about Uncle Charlie and Aunt Kim?"

"They don't hold a candle to you. Mom bakes her turkey till the smoke alarm goes off." Tara put her index finger into her open mouth and stuck out her tongue. "…and Aunt Kim orders the whole meal from Kroger's. You're the best of all. Best cook, most fun, best house…"

"Best aunt ever," Bert shouted, sending bits of partially-chewed cookies onto the table.

Trapped by ego as good sense abandoned her, Amy nodded, agreeing to survive the role of Thanksgiving hostess, again.

* * *

By morning, the glow of her family's compliments is replaced by a gloom growing exponentially as Amy reviews her checking account, trying to match its balance to her grocery list. Shoulders slump as Amy asks herself, "What's best about Thanksgiving for me?"

Without an answer, she heads for the basement, carries folding chairs and TV tables up, two-by-two. By the tenth climb, the living room, dining room and family room offer more clutter than floor space.

After locating extra plates, glasses, cups, and refilling the dishwasher Amy begins her search for space, where none exists, to store enough tableware. Her incoming, ravenous family will arrive in less than three weeks. After placing dishes, bowls and glasses on garbage bags on the floor in dining room corners, Amy slides garbage bags over each stack. Bent over, Amy doesn't hear Joe walk up behind her.

"Halloween's over Amy, why are tombstones in the corners?" Joe chuckles and gives her butt a light pinch.

Amy's narrow-eyed scowl removes his grin. He shrugs and makes a quick exit, mimicking Amy's words from last year:

"Never again. We're not having Thanksgiving here until all of them take a turn."

He peeks around the doorframe and winks.

Her airborne slipper whizzes past him.

He exits, repeating last year's remark, still laughing.

She fumes.

* * *

Amy searches coupons and store advertisements, scavenging for bargains.

"Too much expected from too little," she says.

With the day looming, she abandons the checkbook and gets out her credit card, again, and will pay for Thanksgiving till Valentine's Day.

As the day arrives the fridge, chest freezer and counter tops are buried in food.

At bedtime, Joe assembles a plate of cheese slices and crackers.

"Ready for tomorrow, honey?" he says as he hands her the snack and a glass of wine. She shrugs and downs the wine, mumbling tomorrow's to-do list and sets the alarm for four a.m.

* * *

Amy brews coffee, smiling, as she imagines the delightful family and friends assembly later today. Not-so-eagerly anticipated is chopping veggies, especially onions. As her dripping, reddened eyes blink faster than a Morse code operator's finger can tap, she remembers—"AAAAAAH, I forgot to order pies from Frisch's." It can't be Thanksgiving without pumpkin pie. Marie Calender, Sara Lee and Edward's vanished last week.

As her onion-blistered sight returns, she searches through her recipe box. Amy measures, mixes, rolls crust and occasionally curses onions. Her oven warms the kitchen to an armpit-moistening temp. Pies in the oven, she could relax, take a deep breath, mix herself a drink but, "Oh no" flour decorates the kitchen counters, floor and her. And the turkey is still in the fridge. She commences scrubbing.

Pies are baking. Kitchen temp hits 85. It's time for her to master the ever-unpopular wrestling event: detaching the leg gripper from the partially frozen turkey so its belly can be filled with moist, spiced bread laced with those chopped veggies.

By the time the turkey is stuffed, potatoes are peeled, and pies are cooling, Amy hurries to shove the turkey into the oven.

Fingers lathered in dressing, mop in hand and—hours before guests were invited to arrive—she hears:

"Hey Mom, they're here."

More rabid than Black Friday shoppers, the guests rush through the front door, brandishing their contribution to today's feast— empty forks. Amy stands at the door, welcoming, trying to engage them in conversation. But no, guest after guest peels off a jacket, hands it over and leaves her, helplessly peeking over a shoulder-high mound of garments as the separation of guests begins.

The TV beckons some as it blasts its parade, followed by pre-football game predictions. They are mesmerized, slack-jawed, eyes and IQ riveted onto the flat screen. Others crowd into the food prep and serving areas — but not to take up a chore. Their mission is to test and improve the hostess' agility. They provide an obstacle course that would make a drill sergeant proud.

For one quick minute, Amy visualizes her enlarged table surrounded by smiling, jovial guests who ooh and aah at the brown and beautiful bird resting in the center of the table. These imaginary guests sit patiently while the host, aka spouse, waits until the hostess is seated. Then with a flourish, he places perfect slice after perfect slice on plates. He hands them to the guests who nod and smile at their hostess in appreciation of her culinary skill.

Unfortunately, reality returns. Now's her opportunity to multitask. She mashes potatoes, whisks gravy, pulls hot casserole after hot casserole from the oven, mixes, serves drinks, reaches over and around immovable bodies recently installed in front of the precise spots she'd selected for each hot serving dish. And yet she talks graciously to her guests, smiling like a manikin.

"Honey, help me bring in the turkey," she shouts toward the TV crowd.

Walking backwards from the TV, her grumbling husband grabs the platter and exits into the kitchen. Amy waits, expecting her lovely bird's arrival. Joe plunks it centerline on the table and quickly retreats toward the TV. Instead of the brown and beautiful bird, the platter exhibits desiccated remains already sliced into approximate servings with leg and breast bones exposed. After several shouts of "Dinner's on the table" toward the TV crowd's area, our hostess receives a response.

"Not now. Games on. Fix us plates. Bring 'em in." Smiles appear all around the table as Amy, not-so sweetly answers.

"Get it yourself," then mumbles "You clod," and louder, "Who wants to say the prayer?"

The table crowd lowers their heads as the "We thank you Lord" begins but is interrupted by the stampede of the TV crowd. Plates in hand, they bob in and out like running backs—between seated guests—scooping, bumping and circling the table. Then faster than a referee can signal, they exit through the door nearest the TV. The prayer nominee continues.

"...from thy bounty. Amen."

Amy gathers serving dishes emptied by the TV crowd, refilling them in the kitchen. Once again, deft and agile as a ballerina, she traverses the obstacle course numerous times until all dishes are back on the table. Unfortunately, the seated guests have already passed serving dishes round and round so that when Amy finally seats herself, she must ask each face-stuffing guest to pass dishes across the table, to her, so she can fill her plate.

As she places her napkin on her lap, Joe returns.

"Ready for pie, honey." He scoops a slice onto a plate, squirts Reddi Whip and vanishes. Abandoning her dinner, Amy serves slice after slice piled high with topping to sitters and watchers.

As she breathes a relaxed sigh, picks up her fork, the chair-sitters stand and vacate faster than bats leave a cave. They make comments like, "Sorry we can't stay. We have to go to…They're expecting us." Amy again smiles her mirthless smile, accompanies them to the door and invites them to "come back soon."

Upon returning to her seat, she eats her tepid Thanksgiving dinner alone, accompanied by an array of dirty dishes, half-empty glasses, cups, crumpled gravy-soaked napkins and linens. Unintelligible shouts erupt from the TV viewers along with demands for drink refills.

Disenchanted, she clears the table. Over and over she asks the question, "What's best about Thanksgiving for me?" She refills the dishwasher, grabs a mop and, standing alongside a suds-filled bucket, she thrusts her fist skyward.

"Yes. I know what's best about Thanksgiving—Golden Corral."

Amy's Pumpkin Pie

Electric Mixer Crust Ingredients:
- 1 ¾ cups all-purpose flour
- ½ teaspoon salt
- ¼ cup shortening
- $^{1}/_{3}$ cup cold water

Directions:

Combine flour and salt, add shortening. Beat at low speed of electric mixer till pieces are the size of small peas. Add water. Beat at low speed just till a dough forms (fifteen-twenty seconds). Form dough into a ball with hands. Divide into two balls, makes two 9" pie crusts. Roll out. Line pie pan with crust.

Pumpkin Pie Filling (One 9" Crust) Ingredients:

- 2 large egg yolks, lightly beaten
- 3 large eggs, lightly beaten
- 1 15-ounce can pumpkin
- 1 ¼ cups half-and-half
- 1 teaspoon ground cinnamon
- ½ teaspoon ground ginger (optional)
- ¼ teaspoon ground nutmeg
- ¼ teaspoon ground cloves
- ¼ teaspoon salt
- ½ cup (packed) light-brown sugar
- ¼ cup sugar

Directions:

Preheat oven to 450° F. Separate two egg whites from yolks. Discard egg whites. Add three eggs to yolks. Beat slightly. Add pumpkin, half and half, cinnamon, ginger, nutmeg, cloves, salt and sugars. Beat on slow speed. Pour into pie shell. Bake ten minutes at 450° F. Reduce oven to 350° F. Bake for forty-five minutes, until knife inserted in center comes out clean.

5 – WINTER

CHRISTMAS TREE BELLS AND SANTA CLAUS

By Patti Kay Emerson

When I was born, my sister, Mary, had already moved out of the house and was living in another city about a hundred miles from us. As often as she could, she would come home for Christmas. Mary was not able to come home every year, because she was working as a registered nurse. So every other year, we went to her house.

I always looked forward to my sister's visits home, especially the Christmas visits. When Mary came home for Christmas, she usually brought several medication cups, which were about the size of a shot glass, and we would use them to make bells for our Christmas tree. My parents or older siblings would punch holes in the bottom of the cups so we could put ribbons in them to put them on the tree. They punched the holes for mine, because in those days, the medication cups were made of plastic and the holes had to be punched out with a nail. I was too young to handle the nails.

After we punched the holes in the bottom of the cup and put the ribbons in them, we usually spray painted them silver or gold. Then we set them on some newspaper to dry. As soon as they were dry, we put them on the Christmas tree.

When I was about ten years old, Mary moved down the street from us, but our traditional bell making stopped because she was no longer bringing home medicine cups from work.

However, we had a new tradition. My brother Charlie bought a Santa Claus suit. The first time he wore it, my parents had gone shopping and he and my brother, Dave, were watching me. They sent me out to play in the snow while Charlie got into his Santa suit. A few minutes later, Dave yelled for me to come in because Santa Claus wanted to see me. I saw through the disguise immediately, but pretended I didn't.

My brother played Santa Claus, not just for me, but for my niece and nephews and the neighbor's children. He did this for about ten years. He actually bought small gifts for the neighbor children whose parents could not afford gifts.

Our custom was to open our gifts on Christmas Eve after Santa arrived and eat Christmas dinner on Christmas day. After Charlie started playing Santa, we didn't even go to sleep to wait for the annual visit. Instead, we waited until he came and brought our gifts into the house, and opened our Santa Claus presents right in front of him.

Then Charlie would go change out of his Santa suit, and he came into the room, he would always say, "I heard Santa Claus has been coming here every year, but I've never seen him." So one year, after he had changed out of his Santa suit, I put it on and went to his room as Santa Claus. Charlie never again could say he didn't see Santa Claus. During the time Charlie was playing Santa, we took turns between our house, Mary's house, and my brother Ivan's house to do our Christmas gift exchange.

Several years later, I was living in a place where we had staff taking care of our medicines, and they gave it to us in a paper cup about the same size as the plastic cups we used in my childhood. Instead of throwing my cups away, I kept them and met with other residents around Christmas time to do a craft project.

That project was to make bells for our Christmas tree. Because we were all adults, everyone did his or her own from start to finish. Because the cups were paper, we punched the holes in them with pens or pencils, then added the string. Instead of spray painting them, we colored them with crayons or markers. Some of us even glued sequins or other small objects on them. I even put an actual small bell in a couple of the ones I made.

If I could get more of those little cups, I would make a few more of those bells for my own Christmas tree this year.

NEW YEAR'S CHILI

By Patti Kay Emerson

Our New Year's tradition started at church on New Year's Eve. We played board games such as Scrabble, Careers, Monopoly, and Clue and ate from seven until about nine p.m. After the board games, we enjoyed talent shows or some silly games that some of the church members made up. One year, we had a race with a few of the adults drinking out of baby bottles. The winner got a prize. About fifteen minutes before midnight, we went to the sanctuary to listen to a short sermon and make New Year's resolutions.

Because the sermon was basically the same every year, about starting over and the phrase "You end the year the same way you begin it" (which I'm not so sure I believe), I quit listening to it after five or six years. At midnight, we held hands, prayed, and sang "Blessed Be the Tie". As soon as we finished praying and singing, we all told each other "Happy New Year". Then, we went home.

Church wasn't my family's only activity on New Year's Eve. Sometime during the day on New Year's Eve, we drank a pop and said, "This is my last soft drink of this year."

That was about all we did on New Year's Eve. Everything else we did on New Year's Day. As soon as we got home from church, we went to the refrigerator and took out another pop. Immediately after finishing that pop, we said "That was my first soft drink this year."

We also turned on the TV and watched the New Year's celebrations around the country until it was New Year's Day in California. As we watched, we would talk about the New Year and our experiences at church on New Year's Eve.

However, the pop consumption, and TV watching were not our most important New Year's Day traditions. That came at lunchtime.

We always ate black-eyed peas on New Year's. The story was that for each black-eyed pea you ate on New Year's Day, you would receive a dollar during the year.

Neither my brother Charlie, nor I liked the taste of black-eyed peas, but we ate them anyway because of the superstition. We eventually decided that we were going to experiment with the black-eyed peas to see if we could find a way to make eating them more enjoyable. Our first experiment was to put barbeque sauce in them. We liked them that way, but we thought we could find an even better way of disguising them.

Our next experiment, which was also our last, was to put them in chili. That became our traditional New Year's lunch. However, we do not make chili the way most people do. We use spaghetti sauce instead of tomato paste. We also add other ingredients that some people would never think of adding to chili.

The Emerson New Year's Day Chili

Ingredients:
- 1 pound lean ground beef
- 16 ounce can/jar chunky garden variety spaghetti sauce
- 1 cup sliced or diced mushrooms
- 15 ounce can black-eyed peas
- Shredded cheese
- Sugar or artificial sweetener

Instructions:
Brown ground beef. Drain off the fat. In large pot, add jar of spaghetti sauce and all other ingredients, including part of the cheese. Stir. Heat on stove burner (or in a slow cooker, or in microwave) until hot. Take it off or out of heat source, stir again, and add more cheese and sweetener if desired. Serve and eat.

Alternate Recipe (in case you can't afford to buy the ingredients for homemade chili):

Ingredients:
- Favorite canned chili (about 16 to 18 ounces)
- Black Eyed Peas (15 ounce can)

Instructions:

Open can. Dump chili in a pot or microwavable dish. Add black eyed peas. Heat following the directions on the chili can.

POTATO CANDY THAT WASN'T

By Patti Kay Emerson

When my oldest brother was married, his wife made candy we loved. We called it potato candy, but there were no potatoes in it. We called it that because my sister had made potato candy for us in the past, and what my sister-in-law made looked identical to the potato candy that my sister made for us, which did have potatoes in it.

When Christmas came along, each year we told my sister-in-law, "Don't buy us any gifts. Just make us some of that good candy you make." She knew exactly what we were talking about and made it for us every year, just as we had requested.

The candy was made with peanut butter and confectioner's sugar. It had sort of a spiral design with peanut butter and confectioners' sugar alternating. The outside was made of confectioners' sugar.

Peanut Butter Potato Candy

Ingredients:
- 2 pounds powdered sugar
- 6 tablespoons melted butter
- 1 tablespoon vanilla
- ½ cup milk
- Peanut butter (as much as you think is necessary.)

Directions:

Mix sugar, vanilla, butter, and milk together. The consistency should be that of a pie dough. Separate the dough into four parts.

Cover your pastry board with a small amount of powdered sugar to help with rolling the dough. Roll the dough out like a pie crust. Do not roll out too thin.

Spread as much peanut butter out onto the flattened dough as you want (I just use enough to cover it thoroughly). Then roll the dough up like you would a jelly roll. Refrigerate and then cut into slices.

ENJOY!

6 – YEAR-ROUND

SUNDAY DINNER

By Patti Kay Emerson

Sunday dinner was always special to my family, but it became even more special when my Mom got a slow cooker. For a long time, Sunday dinner consisted of homemade beef stew in the slow cooker. My Mom started cooking it on Saturday night, and then went to church on Sunday morning. By the time we got home from church, our dinner was ready to be eaten. The beef would be so tender, it fell apart, which made it easier for us to eat. It was especially easier for my Dad to eat because he had no teeth. The first time we made it in the slow cooker, we were amazed that it was ready to eat the minute we got home from church.

A few years later, a friend of my family told my Mom about a dish she cooked that she called "Cabbage Patch Stew". My Mom asked her for the recipe and after that, it replaced the homemade beef stew as our Sunday dinner. Our friend's recipe used ground beef and we made it that way the first couple of times, but after a while we changed it to stew beef because we thought it tasted better.

Sunday Beef Stew

Ingredients:
- 1 to 2 pounds stew beef
- 2 to 4 small onions
- 3 to 6 potatoes
- 4 to 8 carrots
- Beef broth and/or water

Directions:

Use the first set of numbers if you are making a small batch; the second set if you have a larger crowd coming to eat. Peel and cut onions, potatoes, and carrots on Saturday evening. Place them in bottom of slow cooker. Add stew beef before going to bed. Add beef broth/water to just cover the vegetables and meat.

Set the slow cooker on low and cook until Sunday at lunch time. Serve. Add salt and pepper to taste. If you have left-overs, keep the slow cooker on low until dinner time. Serve the left-overs for dinner. If you still have left-overs, package them in a bag or bowl and refrigerate or freeze them for later.

Cabbage Patch Stew

Use the same recipe as for the beef stew except you can substitute ground beef for the stew beef (brown it first and drain off the fat before adding it to the vegetables). Add one half to a whole head of cabbage, chopped up, to the potatoes, onions and carrots.

THE TRUTH: MARRIED TO A HUNTER

By Alvena Stanfield

Golf widows and women married to workaholics deserve sympathy. But no misery compares to that of being married to a hunter. Deer hunters are worst of all.

"I think you're making a mistake," my mother told me after we announced our upcoming wedding. Her advice should have been: "Run away while there's still time." As if I'd have listened. He did have many good qualities. His idea of a good time was not one of them.

You see, the hunting man's calendar is different from his wife's. January is not 'cuddle by the fireplace or pay-up for Christmas' time. It's duck hunting season. The mystery pleasure obtained from sitting in a boat in freezing cold, tooting a quack-sounding kazoo, waiting for the "V" of ducks flying overhead defies logic. Even when the husband hunter, after tossing a dead bird onto her clean kitchen counter, is describing his 'wait, wait, wait then success', while he bloodies the kitchen defeathering and tweezering birdshot out of duck flesh, his enthusiasm remains a mystery.

As January slides to February, Valentine's Day hearts and candy are ignored. If the wife complains, the hunter hands her a long list of other critters on Kentucky's https://app.fw.ky.gov/seasondates/ website and threatens to add yet another prey to his (already too full hunting) schedule. In February, rabbit season is ending. March finds s husband standing or squatting against a tree, playing squirrel-hide and seek. April gives way to fishing frenzy, including a trip with seven other "don't waste cooler space on food. Add more beer" deep sea fishermen.

Being greeted at the door with "Good news, honey, no laundry to do," she knows to slam the door and run, searching for Febreeze.

"Leave your clothes outside and get a shower," she yells as she races past him toward her car, a hand pressed to her nose.

Frogs in May seal their doom, located by their croaking. By June, hunters are on the hunt for places to hunt deer later in the fall. Farmers don't want them. Afflicted with buck fever, hunters can't tell the difference between a deer and a cow. Even brown collies are at risk. Hunters damage fences and don't return to repair them, build then abandon tree stands, and fail to share their capture with the farmer. Even property bought to serve as personal hunting reserves are off limits, unless the hunter's June, July, August and September buddying up to the owners brings a nod of approval.

Once given permission, the next stage of buck fever sets in. Week after week, husband puts mileage on feet and truck from Friday until late Sunday, digging holes to embed salt blocks underground, searching for deer droppings, bark scrapings, musk odor and a likely spot for a tree stand. By October, squirrels offer some distraction for him. But no time for his wife.

In mid-November, deer season arrives. Nothing, absolutely nothing, will keep husband away from his quarry. He will sit in a tree, wearing a plastic poncho, sipping from a thermos during a sleet storm. Last year, it took him from November until May to get rid of the pleurisy, but will that cause him to go home until the weather improves? No. Buck fever keeps him warm.

Once in a while, there is success. Horn blowing, his truck arrives with a pathetic-looking animal smaller than a Saint Bernard roped to the hood. Its eyes gaze unseeing and its rack extends upward, obviously interfering with the driver's view of the myriad of roads he's just driven to prove his treasure to his buddies. They, having more sense, returned before the sleet storm and are lounging at a local bar.

Eventually arriving at home and, eyes wide, arms waving, he lavishes his wife with the minute-by-minute three-day hunt and find that resulted in his triumphant return.

"I hate that you killed a helpless animal, but so long as we can have it for meat all winter," she says.

His litany of the past three days' monologue begins anew, expanding, embellishing, continuing, starting over and over and...

"Please, Lord, if you are going to take me, do it now," she prays.

Deer (or Ground Beef) Barbecue

Ingredients:
- 1 pound ground deer meat
- 1 pound hamburger
- 2 tablespoons oil
- 1 large onion
- 1 green pepper (optional)
- 1 to 2 stalks celery
- 2 tablespoons granulated sugar
- 1 cup catsup
- ½ teaspoon salt
- ¾ cup water
- 2 teaspoons Worcestershire sauce
- ½ teaspoon paprika
- 1 teaspoon mustard
- 6 finely chopped baby carrots (optional)

Directions:

Spray large skillet with Pam. Brown deer meat and hamburger in oil. Add diced vegetables. Sauté until soft. Add sugar, catsup, salt, water, Worcestershire sauce, paprika, mustard and carrots. Summer twenty-thirty minutes.

TRYING ON SHOES

By Gary Reed

Family gatherings instill a sense of what family is and provide a certain structure to life. I don't think I fully understood this until I began going to my wife's family gatherings.

Those gatherings included the Holy Trinity of Thanksgiving, Christmas Eve and Easter. They also included Memorial Day and Labor Day, plus assorted clusters of First Communions, birthdays and graduations.

While my wife's mother was still with us, family gatherings were not just important family events. They were *mandatory*. To be fair, my mother-in-law never said, "God help you up if you don't show up!" It was just understood that if you didn't show up, even God would be of no help.

In fact, attendance was nearly universal and mainly ungrudging. Even in their teen years, the "grandchildren" would come without fail. And then one memorable day, one of the grandchildren challenged the existing order.

My wife and I, and our two children, were the first to arrive that day. It was the Sunday of the Labor Day weekend. My wife's older brother, Jack, and his wife, Patty, were hosting the end of summer gathering. We arrived at what turned out to be an awkward moment.

Patty and her oldest daughter, Chrissy, were seated on opposite sides of the kitchen table. Chrissy was leaving for college soon, and Patty was delivering a thoughtful, mother-daughter warning about sexual mores on campus. Despite our arrival, Patty stood her maternal ground and completed the message she wanted to deliver.

"When you get to college," Patty told her daughter, "just because boys want to do certain things, doesn't mean you have to let them."

"Oh good grief!" Chrissy complained, rolling her eyes and putting her hand over her forehead dramatically. "Could I be more embarrassed?" Her complaint was delivered with exaggerated self-mockery, but at age eighteen, it was no doubt awkward to be lectured on that particular topic in front of an audience.

Her father had come in from outside in time to hear the end of the exchange. Probably intending to ease the tension and deflect attention from his daughter, Jack rose to his gender's defense.

"Well," he said, repeating an old canard, "you wouldn't buy a pair of shoes without trying them on first."

The women —other family units had arrived by this time— objected and gave Jack good-natured heck.

Then, the doorbell rang. Someone announced Chrissy's girlfriend was at the front door, to pick her up.

The implication was clear: Chrissy was planning to leave. This was unheard of!

The room tensed and grew still.

"Where are you going?" Jack asked his daughter.

"Out," Chrissy replied, casually.

"Ah ha!" Jack said, as if her retort had conveyed a revelation. "You wouldn't be going to the mall, would you?"

"We might be," Chrissy responded, noncommittally.

"Are you going to check out the boys?" Jack asked.

"If there are any cute boys there," Chrissy allowed.

"And then what?" Jack demanded, attempting to assert some measure of parental authority without over doing it.

"Well," Chrissy replied just before she bolted out the door, "we were thinking about trying on some shoes."

Granny's Old-Fashioned Sauerbraten

This recipe is from my own family:

Ingredients:

- 2 quarts of beef broth (or water plus 4 bouillon cubes)
- 3 pounds of beef roast, rump, round or shoulder
- 1 cup cider or wine vinegar
- ½ cup wine
- ½ cup sugar
- 1 small lemon (or ½ large lemon)
- 1 medium onion
- 1 large carrot or 3 to 4 small carrots
- 1 or 2 stalks celery
- 1 ½ to 2 tablespoons "whole" allspice
- Salt to taste
- Pepper to taste
- 1 ½ to 2 cups browned flour (see instructions below)
- Egg noodles

Directions:

Pour broth over beef. Add vinegar, wine, sugar, lemon, onion, celery and carrot. Put the spices, salt, and pepper in a small bag made of cheese cloth and tie securely. Marinate in refrigerator overnight (about twelve hours).

Cook slowly until tender. Remove beef to cool, refrigerate broth until fat forms (gels). Skim fat from broth and warm. Cut beef into 1 or 1 ½ cubes or slice. Our family always served the beef in cubes. Most restaurants serve the beef sliced.

To brown flour:

Do this while marinating the beef, as it will take at least an hour. Place white flour in heavy skillet on low heat. Push the flour constantly back and forth with a spatula as it browns. Do not scorch!

(If it does scorch, start over.) You want a nice brown or tan color.

Make roux of 1 cup flour and broth in large pot. Add to hot broth. Allow to thicken. You will probably need more roux. Allow to thicken after each addition. Adjust seasonings – vinegar, lemon, sugar, spice – to taste while broth cools and thickens.

If still too thin, use cornstarch to thicken, but remember it will thicken as it cools.

Some use three to five gingersnaps instead of browning the flour, but the taste is not the same.

Return meat to gravy, allow to simmer slowly for ten to twenty minutes. (Refrigerate if not served immediately.)

Serve with noodles.

7 – AUTHOR BIOGRAPHIES

JAMES BALLARD

James Ballard was born and raised in Covington, KY. He has been writing for a little over ten years, starting when he was in middle school and polishing what he knew when he entered high school. He enjoys fictional stories, mainly fantasy but he enjoys non-fictional stories as well, especially historical ones. Since he likes to switch genres when he writes, he tends to like most genres. However, he often writes, and always finds interesting, modern stories with fantasy and mystery aspects. There's nothing like a good mystery novel with just the right twist at the right time. He has multiple stories written, more for personal enjoyment, with a few that have been published in Covington Writers Group Anthologies. He wants to say "Thanks for the taking the time to read his story. Have a good day."

JENNY BREEDEN

Jenny Breeden was born and raised in Erlanger, Kentucky, and moved to Covington in 1985. She has three grandchildren. She enjoys traveling, photography, scrapbooking, and crafts such as jewelry making, crocheting, cross-stitch, and painting. A Northern Kentucky University alum, Jenny is an avid reader and considers herself a lifelong learner. She's written poetry and short stories over the years, including mysteries, historical fiction and personal narratives.

She joined the Covington Writers Group in 2014 and has been driving force in getting their anthologies published each year. By sharing her knowledge and experience in the self-publishing world through workshops and seminars, she's helped others move forward with getting their dreams into print.

MIKEY CHLANDA

Mikey Chlanda is a Covington resident who was born and raised in New York City. He came to Ohio to attend Antioch College. When Maples (the college fire department) found out he had been a medic in a Manhattan emergency room, they made Chlanda join them. Chlanda fell in love with the fire service, and after college, he joined the Yellow Springs village fire department, eventually retiring as a lieutenant from Miami Township.

His first book, "Maples: A History of the Antioch College Fire Department" is a history of the only student-run fire department in the world. His other books include "Mobile Fidelity Sound Lab", a vinyl record price guide, and "The Heist" featuring Shaeffer, an aging heist man struggling in a high-tech world. Visit Mikey's author page at www.mikeychlanda.com and order his books from Amazon at https://www.amazon.com/Mikey-Chlanda/e/B00BHLJQH4.

PATTI KAY EMERSON

Patti Kay Emerson was born in September 1960 in Covington, Kentucky, where she lived until she moved to Florence, Kentucky in 2015. She graduated from Gateway Community and Technical College in 2010 with a 3.4 GPA with an Associate in Art degree. She was also inducted into Phi Theta Kappa, an international honor society for two year colleges. She has been working in Kid Check at Chuck E Cheese's since May of 2016.

BRAD HUDEPOHL

R. Brad Hudepohl grew up in the western part of Cincinnati and attended Western Hills High School. He has a Bachelor of Arts in German from The Ohio State University and a Bachelor of Science in Pharmacy from the University of Cincinnati. He has worked as a pharmacist since 1976 and is currently retired.

ELLE MOTT

Elle Mott has embraced Northern Kentucky as her home since May 2013. Born in the Deep South in the wake of the Little Rock Nine, she grew up in Oregon and has since lived in the Southwest in New Mexico, the Midwest in Missouri, and on the East Coast. She returned briefly to the Pacific Northwest, where in 2010, she graduated from college in Seattle.

Creative nonfiction writing is Elle's niche. Her current project is her life story. It is a thematic, issue-driven and high-concept personal account at 140,000+ words with the working title: "I Promise to Tell the Truth This Time." Elle joined Covington Writers Group when she began her manuscript's third draft in January 2016. Her favorite place to write is with her pet finches, who encourage her with their melodious chatter.

Reading interests are historical novels and reason-driven nonfiction science books. She is committed to her home town and surrounding neighborhoods through activism and community service. She is a page with the Public Library of Cincinnati and Hamilton County.

Everything she writes is inspired by the woman who most influenced her life; her maternal great grandmother, Violet "Marie" Schmidt, nee Godsney (1904-1987). She dedicates her publications to her father, whom she came to know and love only after his death, Robert "Bob" Frank Wells (1943-2015).

GARY REED

Gary Reed grew up in Covington and attended Holy Cross for grade and high school. He did his undergraduate work at Xavier University in Cincinnati, where he wrote for and edited the campus newspaper, *The Xavier News*. He obtained his law degree from The Catholic University of America in Washington, D.C.

Gary worked for a number of years as in-house counsel for Humana Inc. in Louisville, Kentucky, where he managed the team that handled the company's internal investigations and litigation. Before that, he created the legal department for ChoiceCare Health Plans, Inc. He began his career with a large law firm in Cincinnati, where he handled product liability and insurance coverage litigation in courts around the country.

GINNY SHEPHARD

Ginny Shephard always wanted to be a cowboy, but obvious gender issues and a depressing lack of cows turned her attention to the stars, science fiction and fantasy, that is. She's lived in eight states and recently settled in Northern Kentucky. Having escaped the need to herd cattle, she went to school, including an NEH Summer Seminar Fellowship at Yale University, and earned degrees from Waynesburg University, University of Pittsburgh, and West Virginia University.

Publications include: juried academic articles and theatre reviews for three newspapers (OH and WV); *Study Guide for Teachers* on Booker T. Washington's *Up From Slavery*, publ. by Penguin-Putnam Books; and *Domestic Violence in Rural America: A Resource Guide for Service Providers*, Florida Coalition Against Domestic Violence.

She edited *Gaining Insight Through Tacit Knowledge: Achieving Full Understanding from Learning and Teaching,* by Ted Spickler; South Carolina Standards Project (2002) for SERVE, Inc. Tallahassee, FL; *Pamplin Leadership Lecture Series* (2002-2004), Pamplin Scholars Program for Virginians, Virginia Tech Honors Program; and *Sledgehammer or Memoirs of Fifty Years with a Country Preacher,* by Olive Ober Hammer. NKY author Rick Robinson asked her to be a Beta Reader for his *Alligator Alley.*

Memberships include: Covington Writers Group, Defenders of Wildlife, Greater Cincinnati Friends of Jung, Independence Inklings, Jungian Fairytale Group, LinkedIn, Sierra Club, and Southeastern Writers Association.

ALVENA STANFIELD

Alvena Stanfield is a published author of fiction and non-fiction stories. She has recently dabbled in teaching a multi-media experience in all genres and in screen writing. She attends Northern Kentucky University and is on the Scholars List. Most recently, her interests are historic fiction set in the mid-nineteenth century western frontier. Her novel, Frontier Messenger, is expected to be available through Amazon early 2017. To receive a pre-publication chapter, contact 859-409-3434 or stanfieldwrites@gmail.com.

8 – INDEX OF CRAFTS AND RECIPES

Other Books by the Covington Writers Group

Anthology 2014

Anthology 2015

Coming this November:

Anthology 2016

Contact us at:

CovingtonWritersGroup@outlook.com

and

SeagullProductionsLLC.com

Made in the USA
Columbia, SC
15 June 2025

59443507R00061